Gareth's Guide to Becoming a

DEEP-SEA EXPLORER

BY BARBARA M. LINDE

Gareth Stevens
PUBLISHING

Please visit our website, www.garethstevens.com. For a free color catalog of all our high-quality books, call toll free 1-800-542-2595 or fax 1-877-542-2596.

Library of Congress Cataloging-in-Publication Data

Names: Linde, Barbara M., author.
Title: Gareth's guide to becoming a deep-sea explorer / Barbara M. Linde.
Description: New York : Gareth Stevens Publishing, 2019. | Series: Gareth guides to an extraordinary life | Includes index.
Identifiers: LCCN 2017058104| ISBN 9781538220436 (library bound) | ISBN 9781538220450 (pbk.) | ISBN 9781538220467 (6 pack)
Subjects: LCSH: Deep diving–Juvenile literature. | Deep-sea ecology–Juvenile literature. | Oceanographers–Biology–Juvenile literature.
Classification: LCC GV838.672 .L56 2019 | DDC 797.23–dc23
LC record available at https://lccn.loc.gov/2017058104

Published in 2019 by
Gareth Stevens Publishing
111 East 14th Street, Suite 349
New York, NY 10003

Editor: Therese Shea

Photo credits: Cover, p. 1 Hawkes Ocean Technologies/Getty Images; cover, pp. 1–32 (background texture) Thiti Saichua/Shutterstock.com; cover, pp. 1–32 (design elements) VDOVINA ELENA/Shutterstock.com; p. 4 AlexZaitsev/Shutterstock.com; p. 5 Mark Doherty/Shutterstock.com; p. 6 Ta_Ro/Shutterstock.com; p. 7 AridOcean/ Shutterstock.com; p. 9 (both) Time Life Pictures/Mansell/The LIFE Picture Collection/ Getty Images; pp. 11, 17, 21 Bettmann/Getty Images; p. 13 Gavin Eppard, WHOI/ Expedition to the Deep Slope/NOAA/OER/CC-by-2.0/Kobac/Wikipedia.org; p. 15 Westend61/Getty Images; p. 19 (main) Image courtesy of NOAA Office of Ocean Exploration and Research, *Okeanos Explorer* Gulf of Mexico 2014 Expedition; p. 19 (inset) NOAA Okeanos Explorer/Wikipedia.org; p. 23 Keipher McKennie/WireImage/ Getty Images; p. 25 John B. Carnett/Bonnier Corporation via Getty Images; p. 27 Courtesy of Ocean Exploration Trust, Inc.; p. 28 Monty Rakusen/Cultura/Getty Images; p. 29 Noah Brookoff/Ocean Exploration Trust.

Acknowledgements: Many thanks to the following deep-sea experts for their assistance: Susie Hill, education specialist/special programs manager, Nautilus, Norfolk, Virginia; Katy Croff Bell, PhD, fellow, National Geographic Society, visiting scientist, MIT Media Lab; Nicole Raineault, PhD, vice president of Exploration and Science Operations, Ocean Exploration Trust, Narragansett, Rhode Island.

Printed in the United States of America

CPSIA compliance information: Batch #CS18GS: For further information contact Gareth Stevens, New York, New York at 1-800-542-2595.

CONTENTS

WORDS IN THE GLOSSARY APPEAR IN **BOLD** TYPE THE FIRST TIME THEY ARE USED IN THE TEXT.

THE DRIVE TO DIVE

There are two questions that humans have always asked: What's out there? How do we get there? Early peoples journeyed across vast territories, climbed towering mountains, and sailed uncharted seas. In more recent times, astronauts have left their footprints on the moon. Scientists now live and work on the International Space Station!

So what's left to explore? The deep ocean! Even though the ocean covers almost three-quarters of Earth's surface, only about 5 percent has been explored. However, that number is rising, and you may want to be a part of it. Do you have the drive to dive? Plunge in and find out what it takes to lead the extraordinary life of a deep-sea explorer!

→ SPOTLIGHT!

THE OCEAN IS OFTEN CALLED "THE LAST FRONTIER" BECAUSE IT HASN'T BEEN WHOLLY EXPLORED.

From Fantasy to Reality

In the mid-1800s, the use of electricity was still experimental, and submarine **technology** was just starting to develop. Still, science-fiction author Jules Verne wrote about both of them. In *Twenty Thousand Leagues Under the Sea*, published in 1870, Verne described the amazing adventures of Captain Nemo as he explored the deep sea in the giant electric submarine *Nautilus*. In 1951, the US Navy named its first nuclear submarine *Nautilus* in honor of Verne's novel.

People have always pushed forward to learn about the unknown.

WHAT DO YOU SEE IN THE SEA?

Look at a map and you'll see several areas of blue labeled "ocean." Actually, there's one extremely large ocean. For convenience, it's divided into sections. The Atlantic, Pacific, Arctic, and Indian are the main oceans. More and more, the ocean around Antarctica is recognized as the Southern Ocean.

Scientists have also divided the ocean into layers from the surface to the floor. Having divisions makes it easier to identify the geographical forms and sea creatures found at different depths.

The ocean floor has mountains, volcanoes, hot-water vents, and trenches. The Mariana (or Marianas) Trench in the western Pacific Ocean is the deepest part of the ocean. Within it, the Challenger Deep is the deepest known point on Earth. In 2011, a research team measured its depth to be 36,070 feet (10,994 m).

> ➤ **SPOTLIGHT!**
> THE WORD "BATHYMETRY" ONCE MEANT THE MEASUREMENT OF THE OCEAN'S DEPTHS. NOW IT MEANS THE DEPTHS AND SHAPES OF THE OCEAN FLOOR.

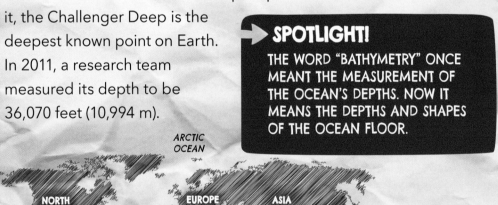

ARCTIC OCEAN

NORTH AMERICA

EUROPE

ASIA

ATLANTIC OCEAN

AFRICA

PACIFIC OCEAN

PACIFIC OCEAN

SOUTH AMERICA

INDIAN OCEAN

AUSTRALIA

SOUTHERN OCEAN

ANTARCTICA

How Deep Is Deep?

In the 700s, Vikings measured the depth of the ocean by tying lead weights to ropes. They dropped the ropes to the seafloor and measured the amount of rope that had been used. In 1872, Sir William Thomson improved on the Vikings' method by using piano wire instead of rope. He invented a machine that measured the amount of wire that it took to reach the seafloor. Explorers used the Thomson **sounding** machine for many years.

ASIA

Mariana Trench

Challenger Deep

AUSTRALIA

IS THERE LIFE IN THE DEEP SEA?

For some years, people thought that life couldn't survive in the deep sea. Otto Friedrich Muller developed the first marine biology **dredge** in 1830. It was a large net with a digging tool at one end. However, it didn't close all the way, so samples from the ocean floor fell out before the dredge surfaced. Without samples, many concluded that life simply didn't exist in the deep sea.

In 1868, Sir Charles Wyville Thomson from Scotland constructed a dredge that closed tightly. Working from the HMS *Lightning*, he collected examples of marine life and proved that life does exist in the deep. Thomson next led an expedition from 1872 to 1876 aboard the HMS *Challenger*. The explorers discovered thousands of new species of sea creatures and found the Challenger Deep.

➤ SPOTLIGHT!

THOMSON DIED BEFORE HE COULD FINISH HIS WRITINGS ABOUT THE EXPEDITION. JOHN MURRAY, AN OCEANOGRAPHER ON THE JOURNEY, COMPLETED THE WORK, WHICH FILLED 50 VOLUMES.

MORE THAN 4,400

number of species discovered by the Challenger expedition

Researching the Seas

The HMS *Challenger* was the first **oceanographic** research ship. Thomson's *Challenger* expedition sailed from England, traveled almost 70,000 miles (112,650 km), and made 362 exploration stops in the Atlantic, Pacific, and Southern Oceans. Thomson and his crew found the undersea mountain range called the Mid-Atlantic Ridge. In the Pacific, they discovered the deepest point in the ocean, which was named the Challenger Deep after them. These exciting findings inspired others to research the deep ocean.

scientists aboard the HMS Challenger

TAKING A DEEPER LOOK

You can't see very deeply underwater from a ship's deck, so how might you get a better look? In 1930, Charles William Beebe and Frederick Otis Barton Jr. began testing a **sphere**-shaped **submersible** called a bathysphere. In 1934, the men made a dive to a record-breaking 3,028 feet (923 m) off the coast of Bermuda.

Oceanographer Auguste Piccard used ideas from the bathysphere to invent the bathyscaphe in 1948. This "submarine balloon" floated on the water until its **ballast** caused it to sink. Later, Auguste and his son, Jacques, made an improved bathyscaphe, the *Trieste*. On January 23, 1960, Jacques Piccard and US Navy lieutenant Don Walsh set a new submarine depth record by plunging 35,814 feet (10,916 m) into the Mariana Trench. Their success set the stage for future deep-sea explorations.

> **SPOTLIGHT!**
> JACQUES PICCARD SAID, "THE MORE PEOPLE DISCOVER THE SEA, THE GREATER THE CHANCE OF BRINGING MARINE ISSUES INTO PUBLIC VIEW AND THE BETTER OFF WE WILL ALL BE."

5 MINUTES → length of time Beebe and Barton stayed at a depth of 3,028 feet (923 m)

Submarines for the Military

Around 1620, Dutch scientist Cornelis Drebbel designed and built the first submarine. Others improved on Drebbel's ideas. In 1800, American inventor Robert Fulton built the *Nautilus*. It allowed four people to stay **submerged** for 3 hours. In 1898, inventor John Phillip Holland launched the *Holland*, the first submarine for practical use. The US Navy ordered six more submarines from Holland. Submarines have been used in militaries around the world ever since.

Beebe and Barton pose outside their bathysphere in 1932.

THE AMAZING ALVIN

American engineer Allyn Vine was a leading scientist in the development of an underwater research vessel that would improve on the *Trieste*. When his dream came true, the submersible was named the *Alvin* in his honor.

The *Alvin* has been in continual use since 1964 and is updated regularly. In it, a pilot and two more crew can stay underwater for about 10 hours and dive up to 14,764 feet (4,500 m). The vessel is able to cover over 60 percent of the ocean floor. It can move over uneven ground, hover in the water, or stay on the seafloor. It has made over 4,800 dives. The *Alvin*'s latest upgrade will allow it to reach depths up to 21,325 feet (6,500 m), paving the way for even more exciting underwater explorations.

MORE THAN 13,000

number of researchers who have used the Alvin

▶ SPOTLIGHT!

IN 1967, THE *ALVIN* WAS ATTACKED BY A SWORDFISH. THE FISH BECAME TRAPPED IN THE VESSEL'S SHELL, WAS BROUGHT TO THE SURFACE, AND WAS THEN COOKED FOR DINNER!

1966: The *Alvin* helps recover a hydrogen bomb in the Mediterranean Sea.

1974: The *Alvin* closely studies the Mid-Atlantic Ridge for the first time.

1984: The *Alvin* discovers **hydrothermal** vents off the Oregon and Washington coasts.

1997: The *Alvin* and French submersible *Nautile* film each other's bottom dives.

2006: The *Alvin* studies **metazoan** life in extreme undersea conditions.

2014: The *Alvin* visited hydrothermal springs off Costa Rica.

2016: The *Alvin*'s camera sled locates the data recorder from a sunken merchant ship.

The US Navy owns the Alvin.
The Woods Hole Oceanographic Institution
(WHOI) operates and maintains it.

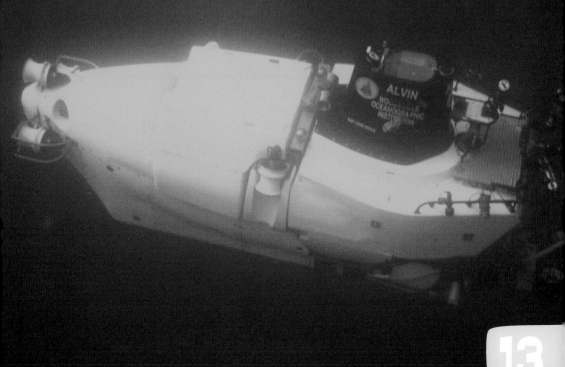

13

FEET ON THE FLOOR

What could you do if you wanted to stand on the ocean floor? If you had a creative mind, you might invent a diving bell. People have been using diving bells for centuries, though with limited success. The bells were made of glass, wood, or metal, with an open bottom. Some were shaped like a bell, while others were spheres or squares. A diving bell was lowered straight down into the water from a ship. The occupant stayed inside. It was hard to breathe, and a bell couldn't stay down for long.

Various scientists added improvements that made it easier to breathe in diving bells. They also added electricity and windows. Modern diving bells use state-of-the-art technology. Divers use them to travel between a ship and their work area in the ocean.

> **SPOTLIGHT!**
> HOW LONG HAVE DIVING BELLS BEEN AROUND?
> ARISTOTLE WROTE ABOUT A SIMILAR INVENTION
> IN THE 4TH CENTURY BC!

Decompression Sickness

Increased pressure underwater compresses the lungs. As divers descend, they take in more air and their bodies take in more nitrogen. As divers come to the surface, nitrogen gas can bubble up in their bodies. If they're too fast, decreasing pressure makes the bubbles expand, which can have effects from joint pain to death! This is called decompression sickness, or the bends. To avoid the bends, many divers use devices to calculate how long they can spend underwater at certain depths.

Workers and explorers can reach the ocean floor in modern diving bells.

BREATHING UNDERWATER

How might you examine underwater discoveries in person? Is there a way to breathe underwater? Jacques-Yves Cousteau solved that problem in 1943. Working with Emile Gagnan, an engineer, he created a breathing device called an Aqua-Lung, or a self-contained underwater breathing apparatus (scuba). It uses a mouthpiece joined by hoses to a transportable container of gas. This gas is supplied to the diver at a regulated pressure.

You'll also need a few other things when you're diving. A clear mask should cover your eyes and nose. A wetsuit can protect you in warm to cool waters. Drysuits are better for colder temperatures. Fins let you imitate a fish's movements. **Gauges** report the water's depth and pressure. You'll also need a watch to keep track of time spent underwater at certain depths to avoid decompression sickness.

MORE THAN 50,000

→ number of Cousteau Society members

> **→ SPOTLIGHT!**
>
> JACQUES COUSTEAU SAID, "THE SEA, ONCE IT CASTS ITS SPELL, HOLDS ONE IN ITS NET OF WONDER FOREVER."

The Cousteau Society

Jacques Cousteau explored the ocean aboard his research ship the *Calypso*. While diving, Cousteau saw the effects pollution and hunting had on sea creatures and the ocean itself. He founded the Cousteau Society in the 1970s to help protect the ocean. His many films, television shows, and books got people interested in the ocean environment and in scuba diving. Cousteau earned many awards for his work and died in 1997. The Cousteau Society carries on his work today.

Jacques-Yves Cousteau—often just called Jacques Cousteau—is known as "the father of scuba diving."

ROVING ROVs

Do you play video games? Your skills with a game controller may come in handy for your deep-sea exploring career. Sometimes, you may be in charge of a remotely operated vehicle (ROV). This unmanned underwater robot is connected to a ship by a series of cables. ROVs can dive deeper and stay underwater longer than manned vehicles.

The *Deep Discoverer* is an ROV that operates from the ship *Okeanos Explorer*, which belongs to the National Oceanic and Atmospheric Administration (NOAA). This ROV has descended 3.7 miles (6 km), exploring areas that were never before accessible.

ROPOS (Remotely Operated Platform for Ocean Science) is another ROV. Its tools can do all sorts of jobs, including collecting deep-sea creatures and cutting through rock. Many of its instruments can be changed for different tasks.

SPOTLIGHT!

THE NOAA WEBSITE OFFERS LIVE FEEDS OF MANY DIVES. ANYONE WHO'S INTERESTED CAN GO ONLINE AND WATCH THESE EXCITING ADVENTURES.

ROV Skills

Operating an ROV takes many skilled people, including mechanical, electrical, and software engineers. The ROPOS requires at least four people on a mission. The pilot keeps track of the speed, depth, positioning, and location of the vessel. A manipulator operator uses the tools on the ROV to get samples. A data or event logger takes notes during the dive. A scientist directs the entire mission. Which of these jobs would you like?

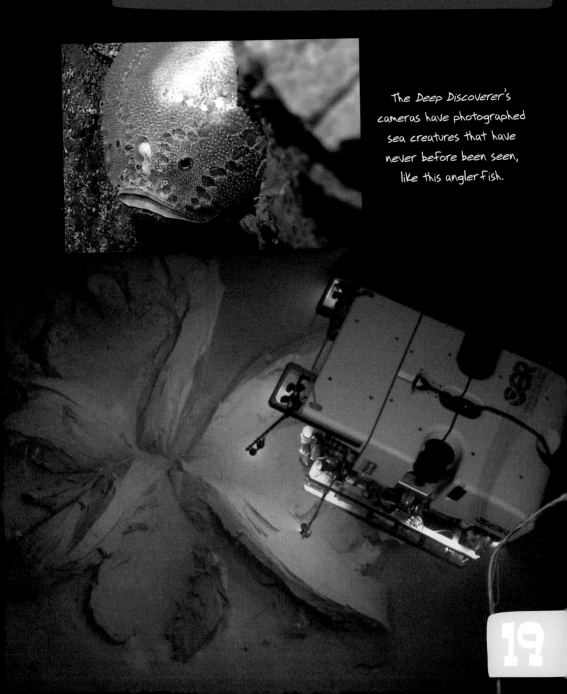

The *Deep Discoverer's* cameras have photographed sea creatures that have never before been seen, like this anglerfish.

SYLVIA EARLE'S AMAZING LIFE

If you want to be a deep-sea explorer, there are men and women to inspire you. Sylvia Earle has led over 50 deep-sea expeditions all around the globe. In 1970, she and a four-woman crew lived for 2 weeks in the Tektite 2 underwater laboratory. Their work gave scientists a better understanding of how the human body functions underwater. In 1979, Earle made history again when she walked on the ocean floor for 2.5 hours at a depth of 1,250 feet (381 m), with just a communication line connecting her to her ship.

Earle went on to become the NOAA's chief scientist and an explorer in residence at the National Geographic Society. Today, she dedicates her time to projects that protect the marine environment.

OVER 7,000 → hours Sylvia Earle has spent underwater

> **SPOTLIGHT!**
> EARLE HAS BEEN JOKINGLY CALLED "HER DEEPNESS" AND THE "STURGEON GENERAL." (A STURGEON IS A TYPE OF FISH.)

Presidential Praise

In 2006, President George W. Bush created the Papahānaumokuākea Marine National Monument in Hawaii. In 2016, President Barack Obama expanded it so it became the largest protected marine area in the world. President Obama met Sylvia Earle and praised her work. "I am in awe of anybody who has done so much for ocean conservation," he said. While about 4 percent of the ocean is protected today, Earle hopes to increase that to 20 percent by 2020.

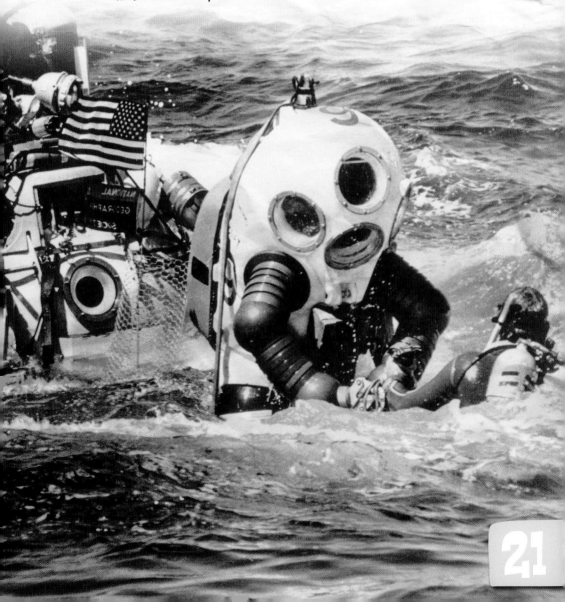

The "JIM suit" that Earle wore for her historic 1979 walk lets divers stay underwater without fear of decompression.

JAMES CAMERON'S DEEPEST CHALLENGE

You may have seen some of James Cameron's movies about the *Titanic* and other shipwrecks. But you probably didn't know what he did to get some of the underwater scenes. He himself made many dives during filming and shot scenes at the wrecks. To do this, he and his team developed new underwater cameras and ROVs.

On March 25, 2012, Cameron began the most exciting journey of his life. Aboard the submersible called the *Deepsea Challenger*, he became the first person to make a solo dive to the Challenger Deep. He brought back samples and video recordings of new sea creatures. Cameron made a movie of his experience to encourage and support the work of undersea scientific exploration.

> **→ SPOTLIGHT!**
> CAMERON MADE THE JOURNEY INTO THE MARIANA TRENCH IN A SPACE 43 INCHES (109 CM) WIDE. HE COULDN'T EVEN STRETCH OUT HIS ARMS!

After the Dive

James Cameron and his team presented the findings from the *Deepsea Challenger* dive at several scientific conferences. Many scientists continue to review the data. They're still identifying new species and learning more about the seafloor. In 2014, Cameron released a film called *Deepsea Challenge 3D*. He has also partnered with WHOI to conduct more research. He's working with their Center for Marine Robotics to develop new technology for deep-sea research.

2 HOURS, 36 MINUTES

→ time of James Cameron's descent into Challenger Deep

In the *Deepsea Challenger*, James Cameron traveled into the ocean's hadopelagic zone—the ocean's deepest level, below 20,000 feet (6,096 m).

ROBERT BALLARD, EXTRAORDINARY EXPLORER

Who found the wreck of the *Titanic*? Who discovered the sunken remains of the oldest ship ever found? Who located the first deep-sea hydrothermal vents? One man is the answer to all these questions: Dr. Robert Ballard.

Ballard, a scientist and former commander in the US Naval Reserve, worked at WHOI for 30 years. He has participated in more than 150 deep-sea expeditions. Besides the *Titanic*, he helped locate the German battleship *Bismarck*, the US aircraft carrier *Yorktown*, and the boat that John F. Kennedy commanded in World War II, *PT-109*.

One of Ballard's main interests is helping children become interested in science. He was a pioneer of a technology called "telepresence" that lets students—as well as scientists—watch ocean explorations from their classrooms. Ballard has written books and starred in TV shows about the deep ocean.

> **SPOTLIGHT!**
> BALLARD SAID HE "GREW UP WANTING TO BE CAPTAIN NEMO FROM *TWENTY THOUSAND LEAGUES UNDER THE SEA.*"

The Ocean Exploration Trust

In 2008, Ballard founded the Ocean Exploration Trust. Its goals include investigating the ocean and creating new technologies. Scientists can go along on expeditions on its research ship *Nautilus* or use telepresence to participate from home. The Trust's Corps of Exploration is a group of scientists, engineers, teachers, and students from all over the world. They work together "to serve as STEM role models for the next generation of scientists, engineers, and educators."

In 1996, Ballard received an award from the National Geographic Society for "extraordinary accomplishments in coaxing science from the world's oceans and engaging students in the wonder of science."

STARTING YOUR JOURNEY

You can lay the groundwork for your career now in your STEM, reading, and writing classes. Two deep-sea explorers have offered a look into how they achieved their dream job:

Dr. Nicole Raineault of the Ocean Exploration Trust took science and math courses in high school and college. These were the foundation for her later education. She studied geology and physical oceanography in graduate school. Raineault said it's also important to learn computer programming and geographic information systems (GIS). She adds that "learning about technology to gather information and tools to **analyze** data is important because much of the ocean is not visible without technology. Writing and verbal communication skills are also important for presenting discoveries." Raineault is now the vice president of Exploration and Science Operations at the Ocean Exploration Trust.

> ➡ **SPOTLIGHT!**
> FOLLOW DEEP-SEA EXPLORERS' MISSIONS ONLINE BY READING RESEARCH ARTICLES, VIEWING VIDEOS OF DIVES, AND LISTENING TO TED TALKS AND OTHER PRESENTATIONS. READ BIOGRAPHIES OF FAMOUS DEEP-SEA EXPLORERS AS WELL AS NONFICTION BOOKS ABOUT SEA LIFE.

Meet Dr. Raineault

As a child, Raineault enjoyed digging in the sand to look at the layers. Later, books by Dr. Robert Ballard inspired her to become an ocean explorer—even though she sometimes has seasickness! Today, she's responsible for the scientific expeditions of the research vessel *Nautilus*. Raineault is always amazed by the underwater discoveries of the ROV dives. On one dive, her team discovered a new species of purple snail!

Raineault reminds students: "Don't be afraid of challenges! It will take effort and work to achieve your dreams, but it's worth the effort."

Dr. Katy Croff Bell of the National Geographic Society and the MIT Media Lab says she was swimming and jumping off the diving board before she could walk! In high school, she took scuba lessons and was a counselor at a watersports camp. Early in her career, she worked for several companies. Her advice about jobs and **internships** is to "try something new—if you don't like it, then you know and you can explore other things. If you do like it, then you can pursue that direction further!"

Volunteer at an aquarium or marine science center. Check the websites of the NOAA, WHOI, and Ocean Exploration Trust. These and other organizations offer paid or unpaid internships. A few weeks on a research ship could turn into a career as a deep-sea explorer!

→ SPOTLIGHT!

REMEMBER THE WORDS OF JACQUES COUSTEAU: "WHEN ONE MAN, FOR WHATEVER REASON, HAS THE OPPORTUNITY TO LEAD AN EXTRAORDINARY LIFE, HE HAS NO RIGHT TO KEEP IT TO HIMSELF."

Meet Dr. Bell

When Bell was a college junior, she went on an expedition in the Black Sea with Dr. Robert Ballard to look for ancient shipwrecks. The experience hooked her for life. She has gone scuba diving over 100 times and has made hundreds of dives with ROVs. For her, "The most amazing thing is the fact that there's so much to explore. The next expedition, or the next dive, could result in a new incredible discovery."

Bell says, "Playing in the ocean, a lake, or a river connects you with an amazing environment that can seem scary to many people, but is so essential to life on Earth."

TIPS FOR BECOMING A DEEP-SEA EXPLORER:

> Study hard in your STEM, reading, and writing courses.

> Read biographies about ocean explorers and nonfiction books about ocean life.

> Learn to swim and take scuba lessons if you can.

> Visit and volunteer at aquariums and marine science centers.

> Take marine science classes in college and graduate school.

> Find internships and jobs that help you explore your interests.

GLOSSARY

analyze: to find out what something is made of

ballast: heavy material put on a ship to make it steady and balanced

dredge: a machine or boat that removes mud or sand from the bottom of a body of water

gauge: a tool that measures the amount of something

hydrothermal: having to do with hot water, especially mixed with minerals from cooling magma

internship: paid or unpaid work done to gain experience

metazoan: any of a group that includes animals whose bodies are composed of many different cells arranged into organs

oceanographic: having to do with the science that studies oceans and their resources

sounding: a measurement of the depth of water

sphere: a round object

submerge: to put or sink below the surface of water

submersible: a small vehicle that can operate underwater and that is used especially for research

technology: the way people do something using tools and the tools that they use

FOR MORE INFORMATION

Books

Ballard, Robert. *Exploring the Titanic: How the Greatest Ship Ever Lost Was Found*. Toronto, Canada: Madison Press Books, 2014.

Murray, Laura K. *Scuba Diver*. Mankato, MN: Creative Education and Creative Paperbacks, 2018.

Orr, Tamra B. *The Undersea World*. New York, NY: Children's Press, 2017.

Websites

NOAA Ocean Explorer
oceanexplorer.noaa.gov/welcome.html
Take trips with NOAA ocean exploration teams.

Sea and Sky
www.seasky.org
Travel into the ocean in a submersible, and read about the many types of sea life.

Smithsonian Ocean Portal
ocean.si.edu/ocean-videos/deep-ocean-explorers
Learn about ocean life and ecosystems.

INDEX